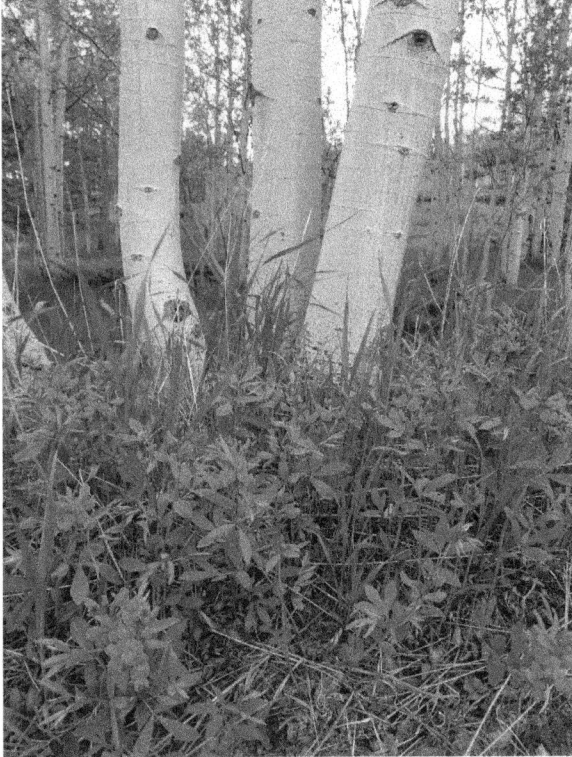

Healing a Grieving Heart
a grief journey in poetry

By David Jenkins

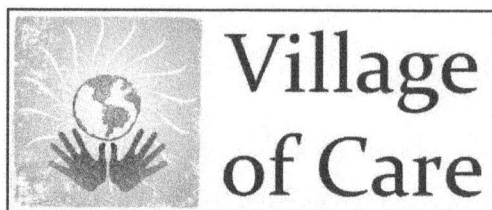

Village of Care Press
"healing the world, one book at a time"
Dallas, Texas, USA
www.VillageOfCare.com

ISBN 978-0-9992588-1-1

Printed in the United States of America
by Hill Print Solutions, a fourth-generation,
family-owned business established in 1925
in Dallas, Texas.
www.HillPrintSolutions.com

Dedication

This book is dedicated to my first wife, Mary Anna Jenkins
(September 12, 1955–April 30, 2017)

Loving wife
Amazing mother
Inspiring teacher
Trusted friend

Acknowledgements

First and foremost, I hold great appreciation to Eva, my second wife, for her unfailing support and understanding.

I am indebted to Betsy Schlossman, a retired public-school counselor and widow, who critiqued my poetry in wonderful and valuable ways. Dr. Tim Bascom, a creative writing professor, helped me write more clearly and concisely. Dr. Alan Wolfelt has long been a wise mentor through his writings and seminars on grief and loss. Amy Lane, who wrote the foreword and continues as my therapist and spiritual director.

Lastly, I am grateful to Village of Care Press for seeing the value of my work and Gretchen Marten who served as my editor, making numerous helpful suggestions as well as guiding me through the publishing process.

Contents

Foreword

by Amy Lane

Grief is a landscape we navigate without a map, where the terrain shifts beneath our feet and the familiar becomes unrecognizable. In this collection of pantoums, Chaplain David Jenkins, Retired U.S. Army Colonel, leads us through the depths of sorrow and loss, offering us a compass in the form of structured verse. The repetition inherent in the pantoum mirrors the cyclical nature of grief, where memories and emotions loop back upon themselves, sometimes with subtle changes, sometimes with stark, haunting clarity.

This book is not merely a tribute to a lost partner, or the heavy burdens carried from military service; it is a testament to the resilience of the human spirit. Father Jenkins invites us to walk with him through the echoes of love and loss, to feel the weight of memory, and to find solace in the shared experience of mourning.

As you read these verses, you will be drawn into the intricate dance between sorrow and healing. Each poem is a step in that dance, moving forward and backward, creating a rhythm that is both painful and beautiful. This collection is a reminder that grief, though deeply personal, is also universal. It connects us to each other, offering a quiet understanding that we are not alone in our suffering.

As you read these pages, you may find your own grief reflected in the verses, or perhaps you will gain a deeper understanding of the silent battles waged within those who serve. This book is more than a collection of poems; it is a companion for the lonely moments, a voice for the unspoken, and a reminder that even in our darkest hours, we are not alone.

Father Jenkins has woven a tapestry of loss, memory, and love—threads that bind the past to the present, the personal to the universal. May these poems serve as a balm for your own grief, a light to guide you through the darkest nights, and a testament to the enduring power of love.

Amy Lane
Spiritual Director and Pastoral Counselor

Preface

Healing a Grieving Heart is a collection of grief-related poems, the result of daily dialogues between my heart, my head, and my soul. They are written following the "pantoum" form of writing, where the second and fourth lines of a stanza repeat as the first and third lines, in the following stanza. I find that this reflective, back-and-forth method of connecting verses lends itself well to the meandering, cyclical nature of the grief journey. I hope you find a friend and kindred spirit as you ponder the poems and engage in conversations with your own grieving heart and soul.

I retired as a colonel from the Army National Guard in 2015 with more than twenty-six years of service as a chaplain and four year-long overseas deployments. Immediately upon retirement I began counseling for PTSD with John Kriss, Director of Psychological Health for the Kansas National Guard. When Mary Anna died, our weekly sessions turned into grief therapy, for which I am deeply grateful to John.

John died unexpectedly in July 2018, which was devastating, to say the least. I had written some poetry prior to John's death but in the following days and weeks I began to write poetry to process the strong emotions I experienced. Over the course of the next two years, I would write each night after a long walk with my basset hound, Penelope. The poems became a form of therapy for me, which my new therapist, Amy Lane, applauded.

In 2008, I began working as a grief counselor for a local hospice, work from which I have now retired. You would think that after working for years with widows and widowers, my own grief would have been easier. All I can say is that, as I began my own grief journey, I knew the importance of finding ways to give expression to the brokenness and pain inside.

Therapy and writing poetry were my ways to process my grief. I continue to talk with my therapist each month and to write poetry, although not as frequently as during those first two years of intense grieving. As I continue working with Amy, I now write about post-traumatic stress and spirituality.

As a bi-vocational priest, I served small Episcopal parishes on Sundays while working for both hospice and the National Guard; I retired from this in June 2022. I still do pro-bono grief counseling and spiritual direction once a week as my way to give back.

I remarried in July 2019, something I thought I would never do. I continue to do the hard and painful work of grieving, but once again I have a life that is good and full.

My wife, Eva, and I have a wonderful life and we support each other, as we are both wounded people.

David Jenkins

Getting the Most Out of This Book

For Individuals Who Are Grieving

Healing a Grieving Heart is a collection of grief-related poems that took me nearly four years to write. It should not be read page-by-page, beginning with the first chapter. Rather, go where you are drawn.

As you look through the table of contents, turn to the chapter that resonates with you. Flip through the poems, until you find one that speaks to the depth of your being. Ruminate on that poem, reading it again and again. Allow it to wash over you and through you. Let it be a catalyst, nudging you to really feel and think about your own grief.

Go for a walk and reflect on what has been touched within you. Pick up a pen and write in your journal or write a letter to your loved one who has passed. Or turn to your artistic or creative side and allow yourself to give expression to what has been touched inside of you. Perhaps, you need to talk things over with a trusted friend or your therapist.

Do whatever works for you, but don't just read the book cover-to-cover and lay it aside. *Healing a Grieving Heart* is meant to speak to your woundedness, for no one gets though grief and loss without inevitably being wounded. Let this book validate your thoughts and feelings, for even if you don't realize it, these experiences are universal. You are not the only one who has these unpredictable emotions, and you are not alone.

It may take you months, even years, to make your way through this collection of poems as you roam back and forth on grief's winding path. Remember, grief has no timetable or script. I also have written a companion book, *Healing Grief's Tangled Emotions*, which may be a valuable resource for you and your grief journey.

For Use with Grief Support Groups

I am astonished by the universality of poetry, connecting strongly with so many people who are grieving. I am consistently amazed by poetry's power to transition a group of grieving people to a much deeper level of sharing and connection.

I find that poetry is like a "feeling wheel" or an "awareness wheel" in helping people get in touch with emotions they have difficulty identifying. I have used many of the poems in this book in grief support groups and in my work as a hospice bereavement coordinator. If you are the facilitator of a grief support group, I suggest three possible ways to use this book or its companion, *Healing Grief's Tangled Emotions*. A grief support group could spend several months using this book or its companion and these strategies.

First, encourage the group to reflect on the common theme that dominated your grief group's last session and select a poem that resonates with you and aligns with this theme. Read the poem to the group after your welcoming time and invite participants to share how the poem affects them or speaks to their grief journey. This may or may not become the focus of the group's sharing. Trust the group's ability to go where members need to go. By doing this each session, you create an opportunity to reconnect with the dominant theme of the past session and take that theme deeper.

Second, if each participant has a copy of the book, invite each person to find a poem that speaks to them prior to the group gathering. As members share their chosen poem with the group, they can speak to their own grief journey and its connection to the poem. You can also provide an opportunity for others to share how they connect with the shared poem.

Third, if each participant has a copy of the book, you could encourage your members to use the poems as writing prompts or inspiration for artwork. This may inspire members to write their own poems. Participants can share journal passages, poems, or artwork at group meetings.

I am certain there are other ways to use this collection of poetry with your grief support group. Use your creativity and allow the poetry to serve as a mirror or a catalyst in your members' grief journey.

Chapter One

Hope Is a Growing Dawn

I remember feeling a sense of hope the first few of weeks after my wife died as I thought to myself, "This isn't going to be as bad as I thought." There was also a sense of relief that Mary Anna was no longer suffering, and I no longer had to carry the hard work of being a caregiver and endure the pain of watching her suffer.

Then the antiseptic of the shock began to wear off. Grief arrived, penetrating ever deeper as the initial months passed. I repeatedly asked myself the first six months, "Am I always going to feel this bad? Is this nightmare ever going to end?"

Yet, there was hope. Hope was more of a thought than an emotion I could feel at first. Hope was there as a belief that my life would get better and the intense pain of grief would begin to subside. Each night as I wrote, I was able to give expression to my pain and ease the intense brokenness inside. Night-by-night, month-by-month the flicker of hope grew into a small flame.

The following poems are from my nightly writings. They speak to a new fallen snow, a wind chime, a barren branch, memories of love, and a sunset that all gave me the gift of hope. Grief is a dark place where heavy emotions abound. Grief is also a place where we can find hope, if we allow ourselves to be honest. Hope is there. I promise.

Hope Grows

Hope grows with the new fallen snow
Quickly erasing any hint of the past
Clean and fresh everything is aglow
The old is gone and a new world is caste.

Quickly erasing any hint of the past
Heaven descends in a blanket of white
The old is gone and a new world is caste
Serene is the soft shimmering light.

Heaven descends in a blanket of white
A realization that life is beginning anew
Serene is the soft shimmering light
Quietly the wind whispers "adieu."

A realization that life is beginning anew
Clean and fresh everything is aglow
Quietly the wind whispers "adieu"
Hope grows with the new fallen snow.

Sweetly Sings the Wind Chime

Sweetly sings the wind chime
To the cold and wintry air
Saying it is night time
Do not howl in despair.

To the cold and wintry air
Its melody softly sings
Do not howl in despair
You never know what the winds will bring.

Its melody softly sings
A clarion of hope in my dark world
You never know what the winds will bring
So much of life waits to be unfurled.

A clarion of hope in my dark world
Saying to me there is still time
So much of life waits to be unfurled
Sweetly sings the wind chime.

Barren Branches

Bare branches reaching for the sky
Stripped of foliage they once bore
Haunting their howling cry
Leaves from them had been tore.

Stripped of foliage they once bore
Empty limbs lifted in prayer
Leaves from them had been tore
Praying rebirth be their fare.

Empty limbs lifted in prayer
Testaments to death's desolation
Praying rebirth be their fare
Longing for spring's re-creation.

Testaments to death's desolation
Haunting their howling cry
Longing for spring's re-creation
My barren soul reaches for the sky.

The Joy of Love

The joy of your love warms my heart
It didn't die when you went away
Nothing can make this feeling depart
It transcends this mortal body of clay.

It didn't die when you went away
It lives in the essence of my soul
It transcends this mortal body of clay
Your love is what makes me whole.

It lives in the essence of my soul
Calling me to find a way to live again
Your love is what makes me whole
It gives me hope when overcome with chagrin.

Calling me to find a way to live again
Nothing can make this feeling depart
It gives me hope when overcome with chagrin
The joy of your love warms my heart.

Forever

I thought forever was forever
Didn't realize it's divided into parts
Nothing can our love sever
Part one, beautiful from the start.

Didn't realize it's divided into parts
Forty-one years the first did last
It was beautiful from the start
Unbelievable it went so fast.

Forty-one years the first did last
Part two is this time without you
I wish it would go just as fast
Is part three the dawn of heaven's hue?

How long this time without you
Nothing can our love sever
Is part three the dawn of heaven's hue?
I hope forever is forever.

Beautiful the Sunset

Beautiful the sunset after a stormy day
Oranges and pinks a lovely surprise
Long the clouds heavy and gray
All gone to my disbelieving eyes.

Oranges and pinks a lovely surprise
Could grief be the same?
All gone to my disbelieving eyes
Can sorrow flee as swift as the sunset came?

Could grief be the same?
Ominous clouds with no break in sight
Can sorrow flee as swift as the sunset came?
I think not, but hope says it might.

Ominous clouds with no break in sight
Long the days heavy and gray
I think not, but hope says it might
Beautiful the sunset after a stormy day.

Chapter Two

Memories Are a Form of Meeting

When Mary Anna died, fear that her memories were all I had left haunted me. Within a few months, I knew I was beginning to forget. This scared me, making me feel as if the last bits of her were fading away. Some of the following poems are feeble attempts to protect a memory. As I look back, some of my writing remakes the past into something that was kinder and more wonderful than it was; no marriage is perfect, and we were no exception. This reworking of memories is normal in grief, as I have discovered in my work with other widows and widowers over the years.

As an Episcopal priest, each time I celebrate the Eucharist (the Lord's Supper) I am reminded of the words of Jesus, "Do this in remembrance of me." The word remembrance in Greek is *anamnesis*, to remember things from a previous existence, and means far more than a simple act of remembering. The bread and the wine take on a mystical sense with the *epiclesis* (the invocation of the Holy Spirit) so that the bread and wine become the mystical presence of Christ's body and blood.

When we love someone, there is a part of them that will always be a part of us. This is more than a memory because memories are far more than simple acts of mental recollection. There is a bit of mystery that happens between this world and the remembered world, where memory really is a form of meeting. I invite you to join me as I take a little walk down memory lane, and perhaps to explore your own memories.

Beginning to Forget

The moon once full is waning
Its presence diminished night-by-night
Its majestic beauty is feigning
Dwindling the brilliance of its light.

Its presence diminished night-by-night
Soon it shall be no more
Dwindling the brilliance of its light
Memories of you share this common lore.

Soon it shall be no more
I fear I am beginning to forget
Memories of you share this common lore
Your voice, your look paling I regret.

I fear I am beginning to forget
The memory of you is feigning
Your voice, your look paling I regret
The moon once full is waning.

Colors Mixed with Yesteryear

Memories of you wash over me
Yesterday merges with today
You're in everything I see
In each thought that comes my way.

Yesterday merges with today
The colors of fall are mixed with yesteryear
In each thought that comes my way
They all make you seem very near.

The colors of fall are mixed with yesteryear
Yellows, oranges, reds—a colorful collage
They all make you seem very near
Overwhelmed by memory's montage.

Yellows, oranges, reds—a colorful collage
You're in everything I see
Overwhelmed by memory's montage;
Memories of you wash over me

The First Time

I remember the first time we came to Red Feather
We got lost, but finally found our way
A snow shower was their August weather
Glacier lakes made us want to stay.

We got lost, but finally found our way
Dreams began about a cabin of our own
Glacier lakes made us want to stay
One of the greatest joys we've ever known.

Dreams began about a cabin of our own
Even though you're gone I come to our mountain home
One of the greatest joys we've ever known
Living out our dream I come here alone.

Even though you're gone I come to our mountain home
A snow shower was their August weather
Living out our dream I come here alone
Today I made my way back to Red Feather.

Forgotten Roads

Traveling roads nearly forgotten
Touching memories grown cold
Dried now all the blossoms
Dreams faded and old.

Touching memories grown cold
Time past long departed
Dreams faded and old
Only yesterday we started.

Time past long departed
Forty years just begun
Only yesterday we started
Happy-ever-after undone.

Forty years just begun
Dried now all the blossoms
Happy-ever-after undone
Traveling roads nearly forgotten.

Our College Reunion

The invitation for our 41st college reunion came today
The photographs really took me back
To a time so far away
Forgotten memories needing to be unpacked.

The photographs really took me back
To a time when it was just you and me
Forgotten memories needing to be unpacked
Happy days so young and carefree.

A time when it was just you and me
The invitation beckons, what shall I do?
Memories of happy days so young and carefree
I want to go, but not without you.

The invitation beckons, what shall I do?
Summoned to a time so far away
I want to go, but not without you
The invitation came today.

I Saw Us Walking

I saw an older couple walking hand-in-arm
Down the brightly decorated Christmas street
Their presence filled the night with charm
To each passerby they'd meet.

Down the brightly decorated Christmas street
Quietly talking they made their way
To each passerby they'd meet
A holiday greeting they did say.

Quietly talking they made their way
Out of Christmas past I could see us walk
A holiday greeting they did say
Remembering nights when we strolled down this block.

Out of Christmas past I could see us walk
Their presence filled the night with charm
Remembering nights when we strolled down this block
I saw us walking hand-in-arm.

Time Rushes On

Swiftly time rushes on
A funeral near Pillsbury Crossing today
We were engaged there and now you are gone
Heavy the emotions under a sky of gray.

A funeral near Pillsbury Crossing today
Beginnings and endings in close proximity
Heavy the emotions under a sky of gray
How I wish our story ended differently.

Beginnings and endings in close proximity
Strange how joy and sorrow flow side-by-side
How I wish our story ended differently
I never dreamed it when I asked you to be my bride.

Strange how joy and sorrow flow side-by-side
We were engaged there and now you are gone
I never dreamed it when I asked you to be my bride
Swiftly time rushes on.

Bittersweet Are My Memories

Bittersweet are my memories
Joy and sorrow flow intermingled
Restless are these energies
A mixture of emotions sprinkled.

Joy and sorrow flow intermingled
Warm and tender a journey to yesteryear
A mixture of emotions sprinkled
Hard the realization you are not here.

Warm and tender a journey to yesteryear
Touching memories forever sacred
Hard the realization you are not here
Times past have become tainted.

Touching memories forever sacred
Restless are these energies
Times past have become tainted
Bittersweet are my memories.

Memories Don't Always Tell the Truth

Memories don't always tell the truth
Time's airbrush takes away imperfections
In an attempt to sooth
Lives in need of correction.

Time's airbrush takes away imperfections
Glossing over painful times
Lives in need of correction
Creating an altered storyline.

Glossing over painful times
Needing you and me to be a better "we"
Creating an altered storyline
It's taken time for me to see.

Needing you and me to be a better "we"
In an attempt to sooth
It's taken time for me to see
Memories don't always tell the truth.

I Will Remember You

I will remember you
Even though the linkages are gone
Pictures, clothes, furnishings erased from view
Changed with the growing dawn.

The linkages are gone
Each one a part of me
Changed with the growing dawn
Misty eyes making it hard to see.

Each one a part of me
Last vestiges of you erased
Misty eyes making it hard to see
Chapters of life now replaced.

Last vestiges of you erased
Pictures, clothes, furnishings absent from view
Chapters of life now replaced
I will always remember you.

Chapter Three

Special Days Are Hard Days

Anniversaries, birthdays, holidays and all the other days once so special became hard. It seems there is a direct relationship: the more special the day, the harder it became. I remember wishing I could somehow erase an entire month off the calendar. It wasn't just the day itself; it was the angst and dread leading up to the birthday or anniversary.

I tried to reframe the day into something else. I adopted a wild mustang in memory of my wife, paying for a year's worth of feed as a Christmas present. I gave my daughter the white roses I laid on my wife's grave on Valentine's Day. I did all sorts of things trying to cope. They helped, but they did not take away the intense emptiness.

The poems in this chapter speak to a variety of emotions. Some poems reflect my struggle with the dread of a special day, others share a sense of joy, celebrating how I was able to reframe at least a part of a day and feel good about it. Each of these poems is real, the result of trying to process emotions and give them expression. Special days are hard. Know that the emotions and struggles you feel are shared by many others who journey grief's lonesome road.

Happy Birthday My Dear

Happy Birthday my dear
I placed flowers on your grave
We celebrated your birthday without you here
Remembering how you so freely gave.

I placed flowers on your grave
Seems like such a small thing to do
Remembering how you so freely gave
Treasuring every part that was you.

Seems like such a small thing to do
The second birthday with you gone
Treasuring every part that was you
To warm memories I am drawn.

The second birthday with you gone
We celebrated your birthday without you here
To warm memories I am drawn
Happy Birthday my dear.

Bigger Than You and Me

Our wedding anniversary is bigger than you and me
Our son and daughter remembered our special day
They reminded me it is about family
Their actions meant more than words can say.

Our son and daughter remembered our special day
Emotions of sadness transformed into abiding joy
Their actions meant more than words can say
Giving me back our special day to once again enjoy.

Emotions of sadness transformed into abiding joy
Assurance that I am not alone
Giving me back our special day to once again enjoy
Through them your love for me is shown.

Assurance that I am not alone
They reminded me it is about family
Through them your love for me is shown
Our wedding anniversary is bigger than you and me.

Special Days Aren't Special

The eve of my second birthday without you
Special days aren't special anymore
It doesn't matter what I do
Forever the day has lost its lore.

Special days aren't special anymore
A sense of dread deep inside
Forever the day has lost its lore
It all ended when you died.

A sense of dread deep inside
I can't stop it, I must succumb
It all ended when you died
I wish tomorrow wouldn't come.

I can't stop it, I must succumb
It doesn't matter what I do
I wish tomorrow wouldn't come
There's no happy in a birthday without you.

Hard to Give Thanks

It's hard for me to give thanks this year
So many things I should be grateful for
Strange Thanksgiving coming without you here
Your absence is something I can't ignore.

So many things I should be grateful for
But my mind keeps coming back to you
Your absence is something I can't ignore
It dominates my thoughts through and through.

My mind keeps coming back to you
Thanksgiving is just another day
You dominate my thoughts through and through
Nothing can take this reality away.

Thanksgiving is just another day
Strange it's coming without you here
Nothing can take this reality away
It's hard for me to give thanks this year.

No Holiday This Year

It's the night before Thanksgiving
There's not a smell in the house
No aromas from the kitchen for sniffing
It's quieter than a mouse.

There's not a smell in the house
So odd for this time of year
It's quieter than a mouse
Just me and the dog are here.

So odd for this time of year
The holiday has passed us by
Just me and the dog are here
Feeling blue and wondering why?

The holiday has passed us by
No aromas from the kitchen for sniffing
Feeling blue and wondering why?
It's the night before Thanksgiving.

The House Misses You

The house misses you this year
Only a single nativity scene is out
Christmas is getting oh so near
Not one of your villages is about.

Only a single nativity scene is out
Lacking is your touch of Christmas cheer
Not one of your villages is about
You are sorely missed my dear.

Lacking is your touch of Christmas cheer
Loud the sound of silence deafens
You are sorely missed my dear
Happier it must be for you in Heaven.

Loud the sound of silence deafens
Christmas is getting oh so near
Happier it must be for you in Heaven
The house and I miss you this year.

Hard to Find Hope

It is hard to write tonight
Depressed is how I feel
As the hour approaches midnight
Your absence is surreal.

Depressed is how I feel
Tomorrow will be Christmas Eve
Your absence is surreal
It doesn't matter the creed I believe.

Tomorrow will be Christmas Eve
It feels like Good Friday to me
It doesn't matter the creed I believe
Your death is all that I can see.

It feels like Good Friday to me
As the hour approaches midnight
Your death is all that I can see
It is hard to find hope tonight.

My Second Christmas Without You

This is my second Christmas without you
It still takes my breath away
I can't believe I'm feeling this blue
My heart says it was only yesterday.

It still takes my breath away
The heaviness is crushing inside
My heart says it was only yesterday
Everything changed when you died.

The heaviness is crushing inside
Christmas is not the same anymore
Everything changed when you died
The pain goes to the very core.

Christmas is not the same anymore
I can't believe I'm feeling this blue
The pain goes to the very core
This is my second Christmas without you.

Merry Christmas

Merry Christmas to you my dear
I found the perfect gift for you
It fills my heart with Christmas cheer
The adoption of Catalpa to renew.

I found the perfect gift for you
You loved curly mustangs wild and free
The adoption of Catalpa to renew
Ensuring her beauty for all to see.

You loved curly mustangs wild and free
Your gift the Wild Horse Sanctuary will aide
Ensuring her beauty for all to see
A year's worth of hay a difference is made.

Your gift the Wild Horse Sanctuary will aide
It fills my heart with Christmas cheer
A year's worth of hay a difference is made
Merry Christmas to you my dear.

Happy New Year

Happy New Year's Eve my dear
Another year is almost gone
I'm getting accustomed to being without you here
The future is coming with tomorrow's dawn.

Another year is almost gone
Soon it will be two years since you died
The future is coming with tomorrow's dawn
My love for you can't be denied.

Soon it will be two years since you died
You are a part of me as the future comes
My love for you can't be denied
No matter what I become.

You are a part of me as the future comes
I'm getting accustomed to being without you here
No matter what I become
Happy New Year's Eve my dear.

Chapter Four

Emotions Twisted and Turned

Grief's raw emotions often interweave and layer upon each other. At times, I struggled to know what I was feeling. At other times, I would feel an emotion and have no idea what was provoking the emotion. Walking with my basset hound, Penelope, helped me get in touch with my emotions and gave me a way to begin to process them. Returning home, I would begin to write. The poem that emerged gave me a sense of peace, as if a weight was lifting. Finding ways to give expression to emotions is essential for processing them and this helped me find a way to live with my emotions. I hope you have ways to process emotions that are helpful to you.

Grief's emotions can be numbing and cold, or warm and tender, or filled with angst and despair. The poems in this chapter begin with the emotion of love. They proceed to touch on the emotions of gratitude, emptiness, regret, anger, angst, and despair—finally returning back to love again. It was difficult to select just ten poems for this chapter; there were so many to choose from. This collection of poetry has a companion volume that focuses exclusively on grief's wide array of emotions. But for now, I hope these ten poems that twist and turn will resonate with your experiences and give you a sense of validation.

Once Upon a Time

Once upon a time
Once upon a dream
The stars in your eyes did shine
Twinkling in the light of a moonbeam.

Once upon a dream
We held each other close
Twinkling in the light of a moonbeam
Your radiance was all aglow.

We held each other close
Such happy times back then
Your radiance was all aglow
Time past never comes again.

Such happy times back then
The stars in your eyes did shine
Time past never comes again
Cherishing once upon a time.

Once Upon a Time, Thank You

How many loads of laundry did you do?
I marveled as I did mine today
Much more than I ever knew
No word of complaint did you ever say.

I marveled as I did mine today
There was the ironing and housework too
No word of complaint did you ever say
Seldom a "thank you" did you accrue.

There was the ironing and housework too
I'm grateful for so many things
Seldom a "thank you" did you accrue
Know the appreciation this verse brings.

I'm grateful for so many things
Much more than I ever knew
Know the appreciation this verse brings
I'm so grateful for you.

It Takes My Breath Away

Your absence takes my breath away
Air has been knocked out of me
Nothing happened to make me feel this way
It's how life without you will always be.

Air has been knocked out of me
Struggling with lungs that won't work
It's how life without you will always be
My whole world has gone berserk.

Struggling with lungs that won't work
Gasping on the verge of suffocation
My whole world has gone berserk
There's no hope of its cessation.

Gasping on the verge of suffocation
Nothing happened to make me feel this way
There's no hope of its cessation
Your absence takes my breath away.

Regrets

I always thought we had more time
Never dreamed it would end so fast
Thought we were in our prime
Never realized the time was almost past.

Never dreamed it would end so fast
Missed opportunities and wasted days
Never realized the time was almost past
Regrets now in heaviness weighs.

Missed opportunities and wasted days
A slave to my career's schedule
Regrets now in heaviness weighs
Please forgive me for being such a fool.

A slave to my career's schedule
Thought we were in our prime
Please forgive me for being such a fool
I always thought we had more time.

I Didn't Want to Go Home Tonight

I didn't want to go home tonight
Empty rooms, reminders of my lonely life
Suffocating in this solitary plight
Deep emotions churning with strife.

Empty rooms, reminders of my lonely life
Your presence made me hurry home
Deep emotions churning with strife
Without you, I am all alone.

Your presence made me hurry home
You filled my life with joy and love
Without you, I am all alone
Absent your look from above.

You filled my life with joy and love
Suffocating in this solitary plight
Absent your look from above
I didn't want to go home tonight.

Feeling Angry Tonight

Why am I angry tonight?
It's been a normal day
Deep within a revulsion of my plight
You are gone, what more can I say?

It's been a normal day
But there's nothing normal anymore
You are gone, what more can I say?
Fractured to my very core.

There's nothing normal anymore
Hopelessly lost, going through the motions
Fractured to my very core
A jumbled mess of emotions.

Hopelessly lost, going through the motions
Deep within a revulsion of my plight
A jumbled mess of emotions
Angry is how I feel tonight.

Frozen in Time

The winter's landscape frozen in time
Bare the branches where life did thrive
Dead the vine that used to climb
Dormant the bees within the hive.

Bare the branches where life did thrive
Cold the wind as the sun turns away
Dormant the bees within the hive
Distant is spring's warming ray.

Cold the wind as the sun turns away
The paralysis of your absence leaves me numb
Distant is spring's warming ray
How I long for the return of the sun.

The paralysis of your absence leaves me numb
Dead the vine that used to climb
How I long for the return of the sun
Here I stand frozen in time.

Another Week Without You

Another week is past
The year is almost done
How long is this going to last?
These waning days of the sun.

The year is almost done
Time keeps passing me by
These waning days of the sun
I've stopped asking why.

Time keeps passing me by
A futile existence it seems
I've stopped asking why
Gone are all my dreams.

A futile existence it seems
How long is this going to last?
Gone are all my dreams
Another week without you is past.

The Sky Isn't as Blue

The sky isn't as blue
The flower's bloom is faded
Sunset's grandeur has lost its hue
The sweet smell of rain abated.

The flower's bloom is faded
Withered and soon to be gone
The sweet smell of rain is abated
Diminished the beauty of dawn.

Withered and soon to be gone
Everything in life has changed
Diminished the beauty of dawn
Even from myself, I am estranged.

Everything in life has changed
Sunset's grandeur has lost its hue
Even from myself, I am estranged
The sky isn't as blue.

All I Ask of You

All I ask of you
Is to remember me
Loving you
This my plea.

Remember me
The love we shared
This my plea
Our lives paired.

The love we shared
Lives within
Our lives paired
Treasuring what has been.

It lives within
Loving you
Treasuring what has been
All I ask of you.

Chapter Five

Linking Objects and Ties that Bind

An article of clothing, a favorite song, a piece of jewelry, or a special place hold amazing power, linking me to Mary Anna. My deceased wife was a preschool teacher with a master's degree and an entire home office filled with teaching aides and lesson plans. For the longest time, I couldn't even go in her office or look at those things. Finally, I found a resource center for early childhood educators to donate these things. I was ready and it felt good to finally give them away, but it took time. The same was true with her clothing, jewelry, and other things. When I was ready, I knew it; I felt a sense of peace and satisfaction that her clothing would help disadvantaged women in our community and her jewelry would be treasured by family members.

The poems in this chapter are about clothes still hanging in a closet, an empty recliner, wedding photographs, an apple pie, a porch swing, a raincoat, cleaning out a closet, a baseball game, and a memory box. These were all objects that held emotional attachment for me. Over time those attachments lessened their hold on me. Now, fewer in number, my attachments to objects are much fewer but still precious to me.

Clothes Still Hang

Your clothes still hang in the closet
I'm in a quandary as to what to do
You're not coming back I know it
I can't let go, they're a part of you.

I'm in a quandary as to what to do
Seeing them hanging there doesn't seem right
I can't let go, they're a part of you
My heart says "no" try as I might.

Seeing them hanging there doesn't seem right
It is more than a sense of the nostalgic
My heart says "no" try as I might
Sacred are these ghosts alive in fabric.

It is more than a sense of the nostalgic
You're not coming back I know it
Sacred are these ghosts alive in fabric
Your clothes still hang in the closet.

Empty Sits Your Recliner

Empty sits your recliner
Positioned adjacent to mine
Paired perfectly by design
A constant reminder of life's malign.

Positioned adjacent to mine
It seems like you should still be there
A constant reminder of life's malign
Amazing the power of a single chair.

It seems like you should still be there
Spending the evening sitting with me
Amazing the power of a single chair
Faint the image I can't quite see.

Spending the evening sitting with me
Paired perfectly by design
Faint the image I can't quite see
Empty sits your recliner.

I Found Your Bridal Photos Today

I found your bridal pictures today
Young and beautiful you are
Memories heavy do they weigh
That day seems so very far.

Young and beautiful you are
Love's blush radiates
That day seems so very far
Never imagined your final fate.

Love's blush radiates
A beautiful bride are you
Never imagined your final fate
Forty-one years so very few.

A beautiful bride are you
Memories heavy do they weigh
Forty-one years so very few
I found your bridal pictures today.

Dutch Apple Pie

I had a piece of your apple pie tonight
I was fooled into thinking it was yours
It triggered memories as I savored each bite
Your apple pie I simply adored.

I was fooled into thinking it was yours
Our daughter did a perfect job, you'd be proud
Your apple pie I simply adored
Through my tastebud's memories did crowd.

Our daughter did a perfect job, you'd be proud
I so miss all the things you made
Through my tastebud's memories did crowd
Even though other things seem to fade.

I so miss all the things you made
It triggered memories as I savored each bite
Even though other things seem to fade
I had a piece of your Dutch apple pie tonight.

End of a Saga

The porch swing rocks gently in the breeze
Warm summer evenings with Sinatra
Chilly fall nights shivering in the freeze
Hard to believe the end of a saga.

Warm summer evenings with Sinatra
Sitting together, feeling you near
Hard to believe the end of a saga
I wish so much you were here.

Sitting together, feeling you near
Simple things that I miss
I wish so much you were here
Thoughts of one last kiss.

Simple things that I miss
Chilly fall nights shivering in the freeze
Thoughts of one last kiss
Empty the porch swing rocking gently in the breeze.

A New Home for Your Treasures

I looked through your pre-school teaching treasures
A lifetime of lesson plans sitting unused
Valuable are they beyond measure
Wasting them can't be excused.

A lifetime of lesson plans sitting unused
They have to continue to live
Wasting them can't be excused
It's time I find someone to give.

They have to continue to live
I can't allow them to die
It's time I find someone to give
I'm not sure where, but I have to try.

I can't allow them to die
Valuable are they beyond measure
I'm not sure where, but I have to try
A new home for your pre-school treasure.

Your Raincoat

Our daughter was wearing your raincoat tonight
It took me back to memories of you
So many emotions triggered by that sight
Never dreamed our days would be few.

It took me back to memories of you
Strange who was wearing your coat
Never dreamed our days would be few
Hard the lump that swells in my throat.

Strange who was wearing your coat
My mind says it should be you
Hard the lump that swells in my throat
I'm more lost than I ever knew.

My mind says it should be you
So many emotions triggered by that sight
I'm more lost than I ever knew
Our daughter was wearing your raincoat tonight.

I Cleaned Out Your Closet Today

I cleaned out your closet today
It seemed like it was time
For too long I had let your clothes stay
Reminders of you in your prime.

It seemed like it was time
Our daughter helped me one-by-one
Reminders of you in your prime
I'm so glad it is done.

Our daughter helped me one-by-one
To give your things to those in need
I'm so glad it is done
It felt right to do a good deed.

To give your things to those in need
For too long I had let your clothes stay
It felt right to do a good deed
I cleaned out your closet today.

My First Royals Game Without You

My first Royals game without you
It took a long time to find the courage
Memories punctuated the whole game through
Surreal it was without any moorage.

It took a long time to find the courage
Behind first base where we use to sit
Surreal it was without any moorage
Feeling out of place, I didn't fit.

Behind first base where we use to sit
I could only look from the third base line
Feeling out of place, I didn't fit
Inning after inning, until there were nine.

I could only look from the third base line
Memories punctuated the whole game through
Inning after inning, until there were nine
My first Royals game without you.

If Artifacts Could Talk

Is that all there is
Life encapsulated in a memory box?
So much more than this
If artifacts could only talk.

Life encapsulated in a memory box
A poor substitute for you
If artifacts could only talk
It leaves me feeling blue.

A poor substitute for you
Changes to our home are hard
It leaves me feeling blue
Disheveled and a little scarred.

Changes to our home are hard
There was so much more to you than this
Disheveled and a little scarred
Memories can't be all that there is!

Chapter Six

So Lonely I Could Cry

It's been a long time since I picked up my old Martin guitar and let Hank Williams' song "I'm So Lonely I Could Cry" flow out of my heart through my fingertips. Loneliness was one of my most difficult struggles, so it earned a chapter of its own. I know I am not alone thinking this, as I have counseled countless widows and widowers over the years. So many times I've been told, "I make it through the day pretty good, but the evenings and nights are the worst. The loneliness is overwhelming!"

I've selected ten poems that express the many dimensions of this loneliness. The first ones are tender and sweet, speaking to a quiet night, a lone goose, and a quiet day. Then I move to the harder aspects of loneliness, bearing my soul about how Friday evenings were the worst and how loneliness was a living hell. The emotions soften once again as I pondered being marooned, how being alone is something I can't get used to, and finally how new eyeglasses haven't changed a thing.

My loneliness did not last forever, but I did struggle with it for a long time, until loneliness transitioned into a comfort with solitude. I hope you find expression for some of what you are feeling among these poems. Know that you are not alone in your loneliness.

Quiet the Winter's Night

Quiet the dark winter's night
The frigid wind is asleep
Nothing scurrying in sight
All the world is counting sheep.

The frigid wind is asleep
Families settled behind closed curtains
All the world is counting sheep
A peaceful night 'tis certain.

Families settled behind closed curtains
This was once you and me
A peaceful night 'tis certain
Longing for times when you and I were "we."

This was once you and me
Nothing scurrying in sight
Longing for times when you and I were "we"
Quiet the dark winter's night.

A Lone Goose

A lone goose in the evening sky
Winging its way, silently it flew
No other geese to hear its cry
A solitary goose in the twilight hue.

Winging its way, silently it flew
Standing at a graveside alone I stood
A solitary goose in the twilight hue
I understood its plight as few others could.

Standing at a graveside alone I stood
Abandoned, a kind of misfit
I understood its plight as few others could
A solitary being totally bereft.

Abandoned, a kind of misfit
No other geese to hear its cry
A solitary being totally bereft
A lone goose in the evening sky.

A Quiet Day

It's been a quiet day
No one has stopped or called
I don't know what to say
But I'm not appalled.

No one has stopped or called
It's hard to be alone
But I'm not appalled
Loving you was all I'd ever known.

It's hard to be alone
Time weighs heavy on days such as this
Loving you was all I'd ever known
Now my life is amiss.

Time weighs heavy on days such as this
I don't know what else to say
Now my life seems to be amiss
It's been a quiet lonely day.

I Miss You So Bad

I miss you so bad it hurts
Welling up from deep in my soul
I can't escape, my mind always reverts
Feeling like from life you were stole.

Welling up from deep in my soul
I seek God's help in prayer
Feeling like from life you were stole
All my efforts get me nowhere.

I seek God's help in prayer
I make my wish upon a star
All my efforts get me nowhere
Nothing has gotten me very far.

I make my wish upon a star
I can't escape, my mind always reverts
Nothing has gotten me very far
I miss you so bad it hurts.

The Hardest Night of All

I'm missing you on a Friday night
Thinking about date-night just you and me
Remembering fun times that were a delight
Life was so happy and carefree.

Thinking about date-night just you and me
How we enjoyed one another's company
Life was so happy and carefree
We fit together perfectly.

How we enjoyed one another's company
Friday is the hardest night of all
We fit together perfectly
Now there hangs a heavy pall.

Friday is the hardest night of all
Fun times that were a delight
Now there hangs a heavy pall
I'm missing you on a Friday night.

A Living Hell

Why is it so hard for me to be alone?
It seems like I should be used to it by now
My fractured soul can only bemoan
I try to go on but I don't know how.

It seems like I should be used to it by now
Distraction and business are wearing thin
I try to go on but I don't know how
To let go of you would be a sin.

Distraction and business are wearing thin
I'm trapped in an inward solitary confinement
To let go of you would be a sin
It doesn't matter how I define it.

I'm trapped in an inward solitary confinement
My fractured soul can only bemoan
It doesn't matter how I define it
It's a living hell to be alone.

Marooned

Marooned is the aloneness I feel
When a couple together I see
An amputation that is real
You were taken away from me.

When a couple together I see
Fitting together perfectly
You were taken away from me
Destroyed was any sense of normalcy.

Fitting together perfectly
A haunting reflection of what use to be
Destroyed was any sense of normalcy
Gone forever the once that was "we."

A haunting reflection of what use to be
An amputation that is real
Gone forever the once that was "we"
Marooned is the aloneness I feel.

Aloneness Is Always New

I picked up my packet for the convention tonight
There was a single solitary souvenir
One instead of two didn't seem right
Another reminder it was clear.

There was a single solitary souvenir
So strange to be there without you
Another reminder it was clear
Odd how aloneness is always new.

So strange to be there without you
I should be getting used to it by now
Odd how aloneness is always new
Stuck in a distant time somehow.

I should be getting used to it by now
One instead of two didn't seem right
Stuck in distant time somehow
I picked up my packet for the convention tonight.

I Got New Glasses Today

I got new eyeglasses today
But it's the same old world that I see
Nothing has been taken away
It's still just only me.

It's the same old world that I see
New lenses made no difference at all
It's still just only me
As the night begins to fall.

New lenses made no difference at all
I can't see beyond this mortal veil
As the night begins to fall
Gone forever is our storied fairytale.

I can't see beyond this mortal veil
Nothing has been taken away
Gone forever is our storied fairytale
I got new eyeglasses today.

Chapter Seven

Sacred Space and Holy Ground

As an Episcopal priest, I believe in the afterlife and I am comfortable living with a bit of mystery and mysticism. I am not unique feeling at times that there is a certain closeness with Mary Anna or that special places bring back more than memories. In my hospice work as a bereavement counselor, I worked with many people who were not particularly religious but felt a sense of otherness at times with their deceased loved one. Such feelings and thoughts are normal. I don't pretend to know whether these thoughts and feelings are merely an aspect of a grieving heart or whether they are "real" in quantifiable terms. To me they feel "real" and the following poems convey a mood of hope and positivity along with a sense of mystery, mysticism, and otherness.

I hope that you will join me in the following pages as I gaze at stars and wonder. As I embrace a sense of otherness, as I see reflections that make me wonder. As I drop to my knees at a graveside on hallowed ground. As I get a glimpse of thin spaces in heaven and the sense of connection with my beloved even on an ordinary day. These poems are the result of a willingness to believe in something beyond explanation which gives me a sense of hope and peace.

Twinkle Twinkle. . . How I Wonder

Twinkle twinkle little star
My thoughts now turn to you
How I wonder where you are?
Above the sky beyond the blue.

My thoughts now turn to you
Yearning, searching, wanting to know
Above the sky beyond the blue
How I wish to you I could go.

Yearning, searching, wanting to know
At times you seem so very near
How I wish to you I could go
Could it be that you are already here?

At times you seem so very near
How I wonder where you are?
Could it be that you are already here?
Twinkle twinkle you can't be very far.

Where Are You Tonight?

I wonder where you are tonight?
On the other side of the hidden moon?
In the twinkling of the distant starlight?
In the soft cry of the calling loon?

On the other side of the hidden moon?
Thoughts to ponder in the nighttime air
In the soft cry of the calling loon?
I can't help but wonder where?

Thoughts to ponder in the nighttime air
Do you miss me as I miss you?
I can't help but wonder where
Hoping that you love me too.

Do you miss me as I miss you?
In the twinkling of the distant starlight
Hoping that you love me too
I wonder where you are tonight?

I Can Feel You

You're still with me at times
It's more than a memory in my mind
A different kind of paradigm
Not limited by space or time.

It's more than a memory in my mind
Not an apparition or a ghost
Not limited by space or time
Of your presence I am its host.

Not an apparition or a ghost
An otherness that's serene
Of your presence I am its host
Feeling a warm tender sheen.

An otherness that's serene
A different kind of paradigm
Feeling a warm tender sheen
I can feel you with me at times.

Softly Sets the Sun

Softly sets the evening sun
Eyes behold the vesper light
Twilight descends as day is done
A harvest moon rises shining bright.

Eyes behold the vesper light
Sacred space beside your grave
A harvest moon rises shining bright
Here I kneel in nature's nave.

Sacred space beside your grave
Something special do I feel
Here I kneel in nature's nave
Wondering how much of this is real?

Something special do I feel
Twilight descends as day is done
Wondering how much of this is real?
Softly sets the evening sun.

Through the Cabin Window

A full moon shines through the cabin window
I wonder if you are looking in on me
Sad the tears dried on my pillow
How I wish together we could be.

I wonder if you are looking in on me
From behind the dark side of the moon
How I wish together we could be
Perhaps someday, maybe soon.

From behind the dark side of the moon
So far are you away
Perhaps someday, maybe soon
I can come to you, forever to stay.

So far are you away
Sad the tears dried on my pillow
Perhaps someday I can join you to stay
A full moon shines through the cabin window.

Mirrored Reflections

Mirrored reflections on glassy ponds
Holding my gaze as if they are real
Seducing me with a mesmerizing bond
Enabling me to touch the surreal.

Holding my gaze as if they are real
Open portals into the unknown
Enabling me to touch the surreal
Looking deep into that which is shown.

Open portals into the unknown
Reflections are my images of you
Looking deep into that which was shown
This is how I remember what is true.

Reflections are my images of you
Seducing me with a mesmerizing bond
This is how I remember what is true
Mirrored reflections on glassy ponds.

Glimpses of Heaven

Glimpses of heaven I saw today
Myriad snow geese took to flight
Angelic wings flanking my way
Covering the sky in a canopy of white.

Myriad snow geese took to flight
Sounds of cherubim in their beating wings
Covering the sky in a canopy of white
Turning my thoughts to heavenly things.

Sounds of cherubim in their beating wings
An artist's masterpiece the evening sky
Turning my thoughts to heavenly things
Imaging you in my mind's eye.

An artist's masterpiece the evening sky
Angelic wings flanking my way
Imaging you in my mind's eye
Glimpses of heaven brightened my day.

A Snowy-Globe World

A snowy-globe world today
Dazzling white accenting every branch and limb
An enchanted fairy tale even with clouds of gray
A soft linen landscape with pristine trim.

Dazzling white accenting every branch and limb
I be a stranger in such a perfect place
A soft linen landscape with pristine trim
If this be heaven I could see your face.

I be a stranger in such a perfect place
Earthen hands and feet and heart and mind
If this be heaven I could see your face
Forever I search but never can find.

Earthen hands and feet and heart and mind
An enchanted fairy tale even with clouds of gray
Forever I search but never can find
A snowy-globe world today.

The Waning Moon Rises

Slowly the waning moon rises
Over the snowy linen land
Frigid the wintry air ices
A glittering wonderland.

Over the snowy linen land
Stars twinkle bright in the wintry sky
A glittering wonderland
Captivating my imagination's eye.

Stars twinkle bright in the wintry sky
Which one I wonder is you?
Captivating my imagination's eye
For a moment my hope grew.

Which one I wonder is you?
Frigid the wintry air ices
For a moment my hope grew
Slowly the waning moon rises.

Part of My Ordinary Day

An ordinary day
No highs, no lows
Trudging along my way
On the outside nobody knows.

No highs, no lows
You're never very far
On the outside nobody knows
How real to me you are.

You're never very far
More than a thought or memory
How real to me you are
Living beyond the sensory.

More than a thought or memory
Trudging along my way
Living beyond the sensory
You're part of my ordinary day.

Chapter Eight

Healing My Broken Heart

Healing is a never-ending process. A heart broken by grief will never be the same. Yet, there is a point where we grow into authentic living again. The dark ominous clouds of grief have passed and there is a reconciliation with our loss. We will always be wounded by our grief, but the debilitating effects diminish. All of this is true *if* we do the hard work of grieving.

I was deployed overseas with the Army for five years of my marriage. In my first deployment, I began writing a letter to my wife every night before going to bed. I called it a "nightly conversation." It was a little bit of "normal" amid the rigors and chaos of peace-keeping operations and the effects of war.

When my wife died, I almost immediately began writing her a nightly letter. I continued my nightly practice for almost two years after her death. I also talked weekly to my therapist for the first two years and then spaced-out appointments during the second year and beyond.

My poetry writing began near the end of my first year and became a daily practice. This brought healing to my broken heart. This wasn't magical; it was painful as I processed the intense emotions of grief. Bottom line: I embraced my grief and I began to heal. I was able to find life worth living.

The first three poems in this chapter are about my nightly writing. Then, I write about "confession" with my therapist. Several poems speak to the dangers of isolation, grief's treacherous path, the helpfulness of meditation, and reaching out to care for another wounded soul. The last two poems address visits with my therapist and the growing peace and acceptance. Healing is hard painful work, but the alternative is to get stuck. The best way I know to honor the love and life I shared with Mary Anna is to process my grief and allow her to rest in peace. I hope these poems on healing become a source of healing for you as well.

Intimate Conversations

My poems are intimate conversations with you
Each night I pick up my pen and write
A way to work my thoughts and feelings through
Baring my soul with each insight.

Each night I pick up my pen and write
Intimate things to you I need to say
Baring my soul with each insight
Seeking peace and helping angst allay.

Intimate things to you I need to say
Soul-to-soul we speak
Seeking peace and helping angst allay
We couldn't be closer dancing cheek-to-cheek.

Soul-to-soul we speak
Working my thoughts and feelings through
We couldn't be closer dancing cheek-to-cheek
Intimate conversations with you.

Between the Lines

Each night I share with you my rhymes
Confessions of my heart and soul
I hear you speak between the lines
Soft your whispers that console.

Confessions of my heart and soul
You warm the beat of my heart
Soft your whispers that console
This was you from the very start.

You warm the beat of my heart
Giving me hope to carry on
This was you from the very start
Even though now you are gone.

Giving me hope to carry on
I hear you speak between the lines
Even though now you are gone
Each night I share with you my rhymes.

My Nightly Conversation

Another writing tablet began tonight
There's nothing to process
Just a compelling need to write
No emotions to address.

There's nothing to process
But a need to talk with you
No emotions to address
Just a nightly conversation to attend to.

I need to talk with you
Just as if you were really here
A nightly conversation to attend to
Spinning rhymes to bend your ear.

Just as if you were really here
I feel a compelling need to write
Spinning rhymes to bend your ear
Thank you for listening to me tonight.

The Pilgrim's Way

The act of confession is revealing
Of a pathway yet to be
What the emotions were concealing
Now the journey can I see.

Of a pathway yet to be
The pilgrim's way filled with uncertainty
Now the journey can I see
Leading towards eternity.

The pilgrim's way filled with uncertainty
A wise sage points the way
Leading towards eternity
Perceiving every word that I say.

A wise sage points the way
To what the emotions were concealing
Perceiving every word that I say
The act of confession is revealing.

Isolation

Isolation is not a form of devotion
It is a prison within itself
An implosion of emotion
Focused upon one's self.

It is a prison within itself
Narcissistic to the nth degree
Focused upon one's self
Blinding the ability to see.

Narcissistic to the nth degree
Cutting off healing friendships
Blinding the ability to see
Discounting the importance of relationships.

Cutting off healing friendships
An implosion of emotion
Discounting the importance of relationships
Isolation is not a form of devotion.

Slippery Is the Way

Slippery is the way
The footing is never sure
On an icy wintry day
The danger is obscure.

The footing is never sure
Treacherous each movement I make
The danger is obscure
Everything is at stake.

Treacherous each movement I make
Such is the pathway of grief
Everything is at stake
I wish there was a better motif.

Such is the pathway of grief
On an icy wintry day
I wish there was a better motif
Slippery is the way.

A Quiet Evening Alone

A quiet evening alone
An uneasiness grows inside
Penetrating to the very bone
Anxiety is amplified.

An uneasiness grows inside
Missing you being here
Anxiety is amplified
I long to feel you near.

Missing you being here
Closed eyes in meditation
Longing to feel you near
Emotions begin abating.

Closed eyes in meditation
Peace changes the tone
Emotions begin abating
Another quiet evening alone.

Tears of Sorrow Dried by Joy

Tears of sorrow dried by joy
When the pain of another is embraced
A healing balm to employ
Whenever another person's pain is faced.

When the pain of another is embraced
A measure of healing begins inside
Whenever another person's pain is faced
A spirit of compassion begins to abide.

A measure of healing begins inside
As I reach outside myself
A spirit of compassion begins to abide
When I begin to focus on someone else.

As I reach outside myself
A healing balm to employ
When I begin to focus on someone else
Tears of sorrow are dried by joy.

A Healing Talk

A healing talk with a trusted friend
Thoughts and feelings found the light of day
Eased it did the dark place I was in
Healing it was the truth to say.

Thoughts and feelings found the light of day
An unpacking of a heavy load
Healing it was the truth to say
A kind of epiphany on a solitary road.

An unpacking of a heavy load
Your death is more than I can bear
A kind of epiphany on a solitary road
Help it does the load to share.

Your death is more than I can bear
Eased it did the dark place I was in
Help it does the load to share
A healing talk with a trusted friend.

Tick Tock

The clocks stopped ticking the day you died
Eclipsed as if the sun stood still
Clinging to yesterday desperately I tried
No measure of devotion did it fulfill.

Eclipsed as if the sun stood still
Days of darkness are coming to an end
No measure of devotion did it fulfill
The hands of time are moving again.

Days of darkness are coming to an end
A new dawn is beginning to rise
The hands of time are moving again
Heavy clouds are breaking from the skies.

A new dawn is beginning to rise
Clinging to yesterday desperately I tried
Heavy clouds are breaking from the skies
For the first time the clock is ticking since you died.

Chapter Nine

Acceptance a Growing Reality

Acceptance is the last of Elizabeth Kubler-Ross's stages of grief. But grief is a back and forth, up and down, meandering journey. Nevertheless, we can see an unmistakable forward movement as we look back over months and years.

The first two poems about acceptance were written sixteen months after Mary Anna's death. I didn't write more poems about acceptance for another four months. Such is the ebb and flow of the grief journey. When the second anniversary of her death arrived, I had written a flurry of poems dealing with acceptance.

Reaching the stage of acceptance does not mean we are done grieving. It means we have reached a level of peace with the death and are able to live forward. I know in the depth of my being that my deceased wife is where she needs to be; death was her final healing. I will always miss Mary Anna, but now, some seven years after her death, my life is full and worth living again.

The first several poems I selected for this chapter deal with acceptance as a reality that begins to grow slowly, like the coming of dawn. You'll meet Penelope, my basset hound. The next set of poems deal with letting go. These poems speak to the hard parts of the grief journey, like cleaning out my deceased wife's dresser and how I had confused my need to love her. The last two poems in the chapter were written about six weeks apart and illustrate a profound sense of peace with Mary Anna's death.

Please do not infer that the amount of time it took for me to find peace and acceptance is prescriptive for your journey. Each person walks this path at their own pace, which will be unique to each of us. The important thing is to stay engaged with your grief, processing it and expressing it in ways that are helpful to you. I hope you find a resonance with the poems in this chapter. If you are not at a place of acceptance, perhaps these poems will shine as a beacon of hope for better days that will surely come.

Just One More Time

I wished for just one more time
One more touch, one more word, one more embrace
But you went away in your prime
Just one more look from your lovely face.

One more touch, one more word, one more embrace
For so long this was my only wish
Just one more look from your lovely face
Bitter the fruit born of such anguish.

For so long this was my only wish
Now I'm more accepting that you are gone
Bitter the fruit born of such anguish
I'm grateful for all we built our lives upon.

Now I'm more accepting that you are gone
Even though I lost you in your prime
I'm grateful for all we built our lives upon
I thank you for the "just one more times."

Open Hands

I still my soul and make it quiet
As I listen to the stars that twinkle overhead
Slowly moves the planet that was resting by it
I listen but not a single word is said.

As I listen to the stars that twinkle overhead
In the still cold of a dark winter's night
I listen but not a single word is said
As I watch for things beyond my sight.

In the still cold of a dark winter's night
Open heart and open hands to receive
As I watch for things beyond my sight
Grateful on this bleak winter's eve.

Open heart and open hands to receive
Slowly moves the planet that was resting by it
Grateful on this bleak winter's eve
I still my soul and make it quiet.

Coming Home

Arriving at the cabin was like coming home
Greeting your ashes on the mantle was like greeting you
There wasn't a sense of being here alone
It was as if we were together, just us two.

Greeting your ashes was like greeting you
It was a warm and tender moment
As if we were together, just us two
Words flow as its poet.

It was a warm and tender moment
I will always hold it dear
Words flow as its poet
It brings back a sense of you being near.

I will always hold it dear
There wasn't even a sense of being here alone
It brings back memories of you being near
Arriving at the cabin was like coming home.

Getting Accustomed to Your Death

We have a beautiful mountain home
I enjoy spending time here now
The anxiety is not as prone
I'm getting accustomed to your death somehow.

I enjoy spending time here now
Penelope and I we do okay
I'm getting accustomed to your death somehow
Even though I miss you each and every day.

Penelope and I we do okay
It's become our special monthly retreat
Even though I miss you each and every day
Somehow coming here makes me feel complete.

It's become our special monthly retreat
The anxiety is not as prone
Coming here makes me feel complete
We have a beautiful mountain home.

Two Leaves Intertwined

Two leaves intertwined settled on your tombstone
Bound fast together by your name they rested
Not even in the breeze were they blown
It was as if there they had nested.

Bound fast together by your name they rested
My mind drifted to you and me
It was as if there they had nested
Two hearts as one we shall always be.

My mind drifted to you and me
A sign that you are with me still
Two hearts as one we shall always be
A hopeful expression of my will.

A sign that you are with me still
Not even in the breeze were they blown
A hopeful expression of my will
Two leaves intertwined settled on your tombstone.

I Cleaned Out Your Dresser

I cleaned out your dresser today
Last vestiges of your earthly life
Sensations speak more than words can say
Forever you are gone from my sight.

Last vestiges of your earthly life
Filled drawers now lie bare
Forever you are gone from my sight
Absent your presence that was everywhere.

Filled drawers now lie bare
Another measure of letting go
Absent your presence that was everywhere
Sobering this reality that I know.

Another measure of letting go
Sensations speak more than words can say
Sobering this reality that I know
I cleaned out your dresser today.

Confused

My need to love you
My need for you to love me
Somehow I confused the two
Now I try to let them be.

My need for you to love me
Kept me hanging on to you
Now I try to let them be
It's given life a new hue.

Hanging on to you
Stifled the new creation you've become
Acceptance has given life a new hue
Still a struggle to be won.

Stifled the new creation you've become
Somehow I confused the two
Still a struggle to be won
I confused my needs with my need to love you.

Tinges of Winter

Tinges of winter in the midst of spring
Empty the walls where pictures hung
So many transitions new life brings
Gone are the days when we were young.

Empty the walls where pictures hung
Empty the drawers where your clothes were stored
Gone are the days when we were young
Distant the memories I used to hoard.

Empty the drawers where your clothes were stored
Our love is making one last change
Distant the memories I used to hoard
Little of our life together does remain.

Our love is making one last change
So many transitions new life brings
Little of our life together does remain
Tinges of winter in the midst of spring.

Rest in Peace

Rest in peace my love
I have finally set you free
It is God's gift from above
I now know it isn't about me.

I have finally set you free
Forever will I love you
I now know it isn't about me
It's time to bid you adieu.

Forever will I love you
Your path is not with me anymore
It's time to bid you adieu
It cuts me to the core.

Your path is not with me anymore
Yours is God's gift from above
It cuts me to the core
Rest in peace my love.

Peace with Your Death

Softly rests the vesper lights
Transforming leaf and branch and blade
Two years after your last rites
Peace with your death I have made.

Transforming leaf and branch and blade
Sacred the setting sun after a rainy day
Peace with your death I have made
Golden light transforming skies once gray.

Sacred the setting sun after a rainy day
Sadness chased away by the shimmering rays
Golden light transforming skies once gray
Hope grows as spirits rise.

Sadness chased away by the shimmering rays
Two years after your last rites
Hope grows as spirits rise
Softly rests the vesper lights.

About David Jenkins

David Jenkins is a Kansas native and retired Episcopal priest with more than forty-five years of pastoral experience with both the Episcopal Church and the Christian Church (Disciples of Christ). He has a wide range of interfaith and ecumenical experience.

David served as a bereavement coordinator for a Topeka hospice from 2008 until his retirement in 2020, spending most of his time doing individual grief counseling and facilitating grief support groups. He continues to provide pro-bono grief counseling and spiritual direction one day a week at St. David's Episcopal Church in Topeka.

David is a retired U.S. Army colonel with more than twenty-six years of military service and four overseas deployments. He retired as the State Chaplain for the Kansas National Guard in 2015. David holds two master's degrees and completed specialized certification in counseling and family systems with the Karl Menninger School of Psychiatry and Mental Health Sciences.

David was widowed in April 2017; his first wife, Mary Anna, died at home in hospice care after a three-year battle with four different kinds of cancer and a brain hemorrhage. He remarried in 2019; his second wife, Eva, is a retired registered nurse. David and Eva enjoy their grandchildren and love to spend time at their Colorado home about 20 miles north of Rocky Mountain National Park.

List of Poems by Chapter

Chapter 1
    Hope Grows
    Sweetly Sings the Wind Chime
    Barren Branches
    The Joy of Love
    Forever
    Beautiful the Sunset

Chapter 2
    Beginning to Forget
    Colors Mixed with Yesteryear
    The First Time
    Forgotten Roads
    Our College Reunion
    I Saw Us Walking
    Time Rushes On
    Bittersweet Are My Memories
    Memories Don't Always Tell the Truth
    I Will Remember You

Chapter 3
    Happy Birthday My Dear
    Bigger Than You and Me
    Special Days Aren't Special
    Hard to Give Thanks
    No Holiday This Year
    The House Misses You
    Hard to Find Hope
    My Second Christmas Without You
    Merry Christmas
    Happy New Year

Alphabetical List of Poems

If you liked this book, you may like the companion volume

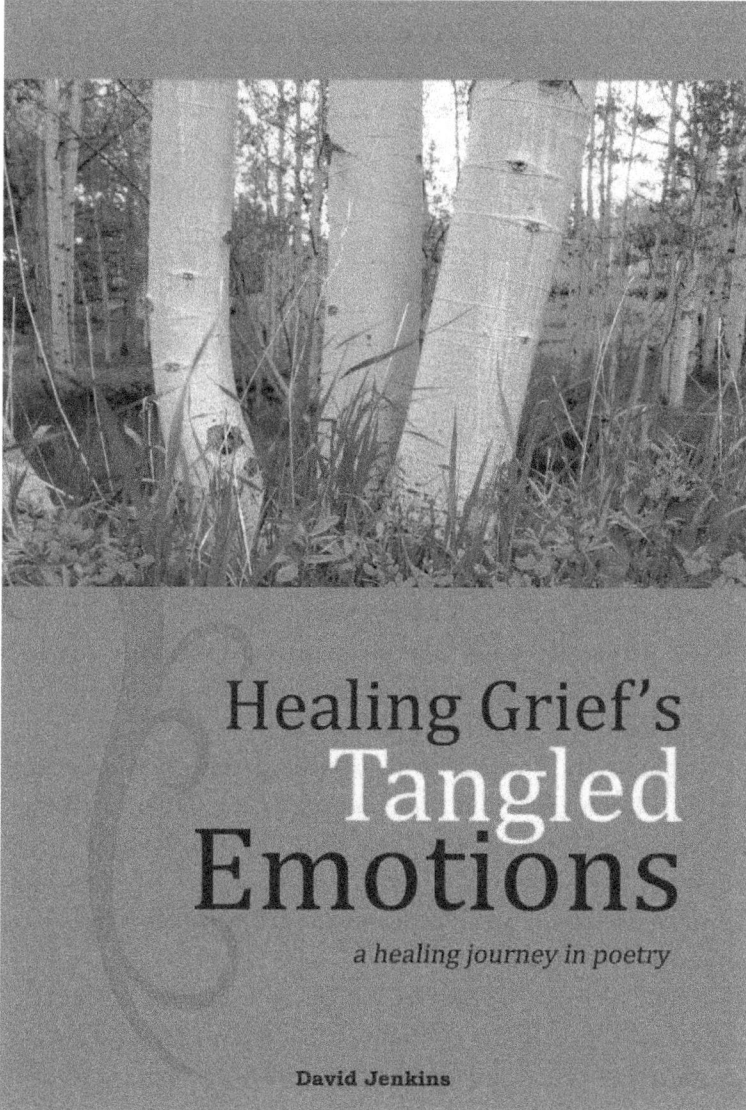

Healing Grief's
Tangled
Emotions

a healing journey in poetry

David Jenkins

Village of Care

www.VillageOfCare.com

Our Vision

All People. . . . Healthy, Happy, Whole

Our Mission

Healing the world, one book at a time

The mission of Village of Care Press is expressed in the Hebrew phrase "tikkun olam," world repair. We believe that we can heal the world by putting the right books in the hands of the right people at the right time.

We believe that there are many authors and speakers with important healing messages who need a wider audience. We work primarily with coaches, spiritual directors, holistic healers, artists, retreat centers, and faith-based organizations.

We believe individuals and organizations should be able to publish books without the cost of larger self-publishing companies and without the time delay of traditional publishers. We believe authors should retain the rights to creatively use their publications free from publisher constraints.

We believe in the inherent worth and dignity of every person regardless of age, gender, race, ethnicity, ability, religious preference, national origin, immigration or refugee status, sexual orientation, or gender identity/expression.

To discuss ideas for your Self, your organization, or your community, please contact Gretchen Martens at Gretchen@GretchenMartens.com.

www.ingramcontent.com/pod-product-compliance
Lightning Source LLC
Chambersburg PA
CBHW032036040426
42449CB00007B/915